Gardener's G
Growing Cucumbers

The Growing Cucumbers in the Vegetable Garden Book

Gardener's Guide to Growing Your Vegetable Garden Book VI

Paul R. Wonning

Gardener's Guide to Growing Cucumbers

Published Paul R. Wonning

Copyright 2016 by Paul R. Wonning

Print Edition

paulwonning@gmail.com

If you would like email notification of when new Mossy Feet books become available email the author for inclusion in the subscription list.

Join Me on Facebook

Search Mossy Feet Books

Find them on www.mossyfeetbooks.com

Mossy Feet Books

Description

Growing cucumbers in the vegetable garden is easier than you might think. Fresh cucumbers provide a tasty vegetable treat for the table and excellent addition to salads or to just eat. Pickled cucumbers extend the eating season for the cucumber well into winter, as well.

Gardener's Guide to Growing Cucumbers is an excellent vegetable garden guide for the garden beginner as well as the veteran gardener.

Vegetable gardeners will find sections on growing, freeing, storing and canning carrots. Planting, culture, harvest and storage of the carrot is covered as well.

Gardener's Guide to Growing Cucumbers contains a list of seed sources as well. It will please vegetable gardeners to find our extensive list of seed catalogs included as well. This updated catalog includes some new seed catalog finds.

The garden vegetable series *Gardener's Guide to Growing Your Vegetable Garden* includes this book. This exciting new series of vegetable gardening books will include twenty vegetables. These are the most common ones grown in the home vegetable garden. The books will all include complete growing, culture, botanical, harvesting and storage information. Great for veteran or beginning gardeners the series is written for gardeners by a gardener.

Table of Contents

Gardener's Guide to Growing Cucumbers

Paul R. Wonning

Introduction

This widely cultivated plant has developed into one of the most popular vegetables to inhabit the home garden. Easy to grow with few pests, diners may enjoy cucumbers raw, pickled and fried. The trailing vines can grow up space saving trellises in the garden or in containers on the patio.

The cucumber requires hot, humid weather with plenty of water to developed fruits. They will also need a minimum of eight hours of sun a day. Most cucumber varieties are diecious, meaning they have both male and female flowers on the same plant. The male flowers will appear about a week before the female flowers. Bees and other insects pollinate the flowers. There are also hynoecious varieties that will produce higher yields. These types will have plants with male flowers and plants with female flowers. You must plant both sexes for fruit, and the male seeds are usually marked in the packet.

Common Name:

Cucumber

The name cucumber derives from the Latin name for them, cucumerem. The origin of this name is lost to time. For a time in Seventeenth Century England, the vegetable was despised and considered it fit only for cow fodder. They used the name "cowcumber" in reference to it.

Botanical Name:

Cucumis sativus

The genus name, Cucumis, derives from the Latin name for cucumber, the species name sativus refers to the cultivated cucumber.

Family:

Cucurbitaceae

Sometimes called the cucumber, or gourd, family, this economically important family includes the genera Cucurbita (squash), Lagenaria (gourds), Citrullus (watermelon), and Cucumis (cucumber).

The family contains ninety-eight genera and 975 species. These genera's natural habits are mostly in the tropical regions and all are frost sensitive. Most of the species are annual vines with tendrils perpendicular to the leaf nodes. The stem is hairy. The plants possess large, yellow or white uni-sexual flowers. The species have male and female flowers either on different plants (dioecious) or on the same plant (monoecious). The female flowers develop into a modified berry called a pepo. Most species have palmate, simple or lobed leaves.

Sun:

Full sun

Soil:

The cucumber tolerates a wide range of soils, sandy, clay and loam. It will tolerate Ph ranges from slightly acid to slightly alkaline. It prefers moist, well-drained soils.

Hardiness Zone:

Cucumbers are annual vines that tolerate no frost during their growing season. They do well in northern gardens during the summer months after all danger of frost has passed.

Origins:

Horticulturalists believe that the cucumber originated in Southeast Asia. However, the cucumber has been cultivated since ancient times. The Bible contains references to it and there is evidence that peoples in ancient Greece consumed it. Most believe it spread to the Middle East through India. The Romans loved the cucumber. They used an oiled cloth called specularia to construct special houses to grow cucumber during the winter months. There were different varieties grown in Italy, Africa and Greece. By the Fourteenth Century, the British began growing cucumbers and thence they came to the New World during the European colonial period.

Propagation:

Gardeners propagate cucumbers mainly by sowing seed purchased from a seed catalog or other seed retailer. It is possible to save seed from non-hybrid varieties of cucumber grown in the garden. To save seed, different varieties of cucumber must be separated by at leas one-half mile. Allow the cucumbers you wish to save seed from to ripen. The fruits saved for seed cannot be eaten. After the fruit has ripened, remove and allow the fruit to finish ripening in a cool, dry place for a few weeks. Slice the ripened seed lengthwise and scrape out the seeds and the jelly-like fluid with a spoon. Put the fluid and the seeds in a jar at room temperature for three to four days. During this time, the jelly will dissolve and the good seeds will sink. A fungus will form on the top. Skim the immature seeds and debris from the top of the liquid after the jelly has dissolved. Spread the seeds on a screen or paper towel to dry. Store the seeds in a cool area. A crisper drawer of the refrigerator is fine. The seed should stay good for a couple of years. Save the seed from at least three different plants to prevent inbreeding depression.

Plant Height, Spread, Spacing:

Cucumber vines height will vary by the variety grown. This can be from three feet for bush varieties to eight feet or more for vines. Spacing will depend upon the growing method used. If grown in a row where the vines trail along the ground, spacing should be eighteen to thirty six inches. If grown on a trellis, spacing can be somewhat closer.

Male Flower

Flower Color, Description

Cucumber bears three quarter inch diameter yellow flowers with five petals. Cucumbers are diecious, bearing male and female flowers on the same plant. The male flowers usually appear first, in the upper leaf axils. Female flowers, with their cucumber shaped ovaries, appear later. Honeybees or bumblebees visit the male flowers, and then visit the female flowers for the nectar, depositing pollen grains in the process. The pollinated ovary develops into an elongated fruit with tapered ends. Most cucumbers need pollination for fruiting to occur. However, some varieties, called parthenocarpic, produce all female flowers that develop into seedless, fruit.

Female Flower

Pollination:

Most cucumbers are not self-pollinated. They require pollination from other cucumber plants for seeds to form and fruit to set. Honeybees and bumblebees are the primary pollinators of cucumbers, but other insects may do it, as well. Commercial growers require vast numbers of bees, but the home gardener can rely on wild bees that inhabit the area. If spraying insecticides for pests, use types that do not kill bees and spray at times when the bees are inactive. Read the labels of the insecticides for instructions on how to avoid harming the bees.

Plant Description:

The cucumber plant is a vine the trails along the ground. Using its tendrils, the vine can climb trellises for vertical gardening methods. The large alternate, palm-shaped leaves cover the fruits, protecting them from the sun. Tendrils and flowers originate from the leaf axils. Short, sharp spines that can prick the skin cover the stems, leaf stalks and fruit.

Planting Seeds:

Direct seed cucumber into the garden after all danger of frost has passed. The seeds probably will not germinate in cold soil, so it is best to wait until the soil has warmed. The seed should germinate in seven to ten days, but cooler weather may delay germination.

Gardeners can get an early start on the season by sowing the cucumber seed in pots in the greenhouse, hot bed or under grow lights. Sow the seed four to six weeks before the last scheduled spring frost, this will vary by geographic location. Check with your local agricultural extension office. A sunny windowsill will work, also, as long as the room stays warm overnight. It is best to sow the seed into a two to three inch pot. Poke a hole in the potting soil and plant the seed one-half to one inch deep. Water the soil well, but do not get it soggy. Place a sheet of clear plastic wrap over the pot and secure with a rubber band. Cover the seed and set in a warm place. Make sure the soil stays moist. The seed should germinate in seven to ten days at sixty-eight to seventy-two degrees. When germination has occurred, remove the plastic. Cucumber seedlings need a lot of light to avoid stretching. Keep well watered, but not soggy.

Growing Seedlings:

Seedlings in the garden need little care except to watch for slug, flea beetle and aphid damage. Thin the plants to about eighteen inches apart in a row garden. Seedlings grown under lights or in windows must receive adequate light to keep them from stretching. Keep the soil moist but not saturated with water and keep the temperature above about sixty-five degrees. Thin to one seedling per pot. Try to avoid transplanting, but plant directly into the garden after all danger of frost has passed.

Garden Culture

Cucumbers can trail along the ground, or build trellises for them to twine. Trellises grown cucumbers save garden space and allow the fruit to stay cleaner. Water cucumbers often, as ample water supplies will encourage greater fruit production. About one-half inch of rain is best for good production. Drip irrigation is the best, as wetting foliage can spread diseases. A water-filled jug with a tiny hole poked in the bottom and placed by the plant will provide a slow, steady application of water as the water leaks out. Tall tomato cages also make good cucumber trellises. Bush varieties do not need trellises. Fertilize the soil prior to planting with rich compost, worm castings or well rotted manure. Manure applications are best applied in the autumn. If using chemical fertilizers, apply some 10-10-10 or 12-12-12 fertilizer at planting. An additional, light application when the plant begins to bloom may be beneficial. Do not overdo or you can burn the plants. You may also mix a water-soluble fertilizer in the water when irrigating. If using the jug system, just fill the jugs, put in the recommended dosage of fertilizer and water as usual.

Problems:

Angular leaf spot

Bacteria - Pseudomonas syringae

Symptoms:

There are small water-soaked lesions on the leaves that expand between the leaf veins and become angular in shape. During high humidity conditions, the lesions may exude a milky substance that dries to form a white crust on or beside the lesions. As the disease progresses, the lesions will turn tan and may have yellow edges. The centers of the lesions will dry and may drop out leaving a hole in the leaf.

This disease spreads through infected seed, rain, insects and the movement of people between plants. The bacterium over winters in crop debris and can survive for three years in the soil.

Treatment:

Use disease-free seed. Rotate cucurbits every two years. Copper spray may help reduce incidence of disease in warm, humid climates. Plant resistant varieties

Bacterial wilt

Bacteria - Erwinia tracheiphila

Symptoms:

The plant begins to wilt and rapidly die. Infected runners will appear dark green in but rapidly become necrotic as the disease progresses

This disease can result in heavy crop losses. The striped or spotted cucumber beetles spread the disease. To confirm the disease, cut the stem and pull the two ends apart. Infected plants will ooze.

Treatment:

Control cucumber beetles by hand picking the adult beetles. Foliar application of appropriate insecticides may help to control the insects.

Anthracnose

Fungus - Colletotrichum orbiculare

Symptoms

The leaves will develop brown circular lesions with yellow edges. The petioles, stems and fruit; lesions on resistant varieties appear tan with green edges. The lesions will dry out and drop out of leaves

This disease favors warm temperatures

Treatment:

Plant only resistant varieties in the garden and use only certified seed. Fungicides can stop the spread the disease. Rotate crops every year.

Belly rot (Fruit rot, Damping-off)

Fungus - Rhizoctonia solani

The fruit will develop a yellow-brown discoloration. It develops water soaked spots on sides of fruit in contact with soil. brown mold growing on rotting areas; collapse of seedlings

The disease favors warm, humid conditions.

Treatment:

Till the soil deep before to planting and use plastic mulch to create a barrier between the fruit and soil. Plant them in well-drained sites. Apply fungicides when plants begin to vine.

Downy mildew

Fungus - Pseudoperonospora cubensis

Symptoms

Fluffy purple mildew grows on the underside of the leaves. Yellow spots form on the upper side of leaves. The disease favors cool, humid conditions.

Treatment:

Do not overcrowd the plants and avoid overhead irrigation. Use drip irrigation or water plants from the base. Apply appropriate fungicides when the disease develops.

Fusarium wilt (Cucumber wilt, Foot-rot)

Fungus - Fusarium oxysporum

Symptoms:

The seedlings will rot at the soil line. Brown lesions form on one side of the stem.

Treatment:

The disease favors warm, moist soil. Use a fungicide treated seed and rotate crops on 4 year cycle.

Gummy stem blight

Fungus - Mycosphaerella melonis

This disease appears Gray-green lesions between veins of leaves and tan or gray lesions on the stems.

The disease may be seed-borne.

Treatment:

Use disease free seed or treat seeds prior to planting with a fungicide. Rotate crops every two years.

Target leaf spot

Fungus - Corynespora cassiicola

Fungus - Corynespora. melonis

Symptoms:

Angular yellow spots will appear on older leaves. As the disease progresses, the spots enlarge and become circular with light brown centers and dark margins. The lesions mature, turn gray and drop out leaving holes in the leaves. If the fruits become infected early in their growth then the blossom end may darken and shrivel. The fungus can survive on plant debris for periods in excess of two years. Periods of high humidity and temperature allow the disease to emerge.

Treatment:

Plant resistant varieties and apply fungicides. Sanitize equipment regularly to kill the fungus.

Cucumber mosaic

Cucumber mosaic virus (CMV on Seed Packets)

Symptoms

Plants are severely stunted and the foliage is covered in distinctive yellow mosaic. The leaves of the plant will curl down and the leaf size is smaller than normal. The flowers on infected plants may be deformed and have green petals. The fruits become distorted and small. Mosaic will sometimes cause discolored fruit. Aphids transmit mosaic. The virus has an extensive host range. Infected tools, hands can spread the virus.

Treatment:

Control aphids to control the disease. Reflective mulches can deter aphids. Treat aphids with mineral oils or insecticidal soap. There are some resistant varieties are available

Cucumber beetles (Western striped cucumber beetle, Western spotted cucumber beetle, Banded cucumber beetle)

Acalymma vittata

Diabrotica undecimpunctata

Diabrotica balteata

These insects cause stunted seedlings and damaged leaves. The stems may exhibit symptoms of bacterial wilt. Scars appear on the fruit caused by the beetles feeding. Adult beetles are brightly colored with either a green-yellow background and black spots or alternating black and yellow stripes

Treatment:

Beetles over winter in soil and leaf litter. They emerge from soil when temperatures begin to reach and exceed 55°F. Monitor new planting regularly for signs of beetle. Use floating row covers to protect the plants from damage. These need removal when the plants bloom to allow bees to pollinate plants. Use insects to control the insects.

Cabbage looper

Trichoplusia ni

Symptoms

These caterpillars chew large or small holes in the leaves and damage soften extensive. The caterpillars are pale green with white lines running down either side of their body. These caterpillars their body when they move. The adults lay single eggs, usually on the lower leaf surface close to the leaf margin. The eggs are white or pale green.

The pupae survive over the winter as pupae in crop debris. The adult insect is a dark colored moth and the caterpillars have a wide host range, including most cabbage crops.

Treatment

Natural enemies like birds and wasps usually keep the looper population in check. Hand pick the loopers from the plant. Bacillus thuringiensis kills younger larvae. Chemical sprays may damage populations of natural enemies and bees. Use these carefully.

Flea beetles

Epitrix spp.

Symptoms

These tiny insects chew small holes in the leaves that give the foliage a characteristic "shot hole" appearance. Young plants and seedlings are particularly susceptible. The damage may stunt plant growth. Severe damage can kill the plant. Flea beetles are tiny, pin head sized insects. They are usually black and jump like fleas when disturbed.

Flea beetles may over winter on nearby weeds, in plant debris or in the soil. The insects can produce two or three generations in one season.

Treatment:

Floating row covers may a physical barrier to protect young plants before the beetles emerge in the spring. Plant the seeds early to allow them to become established before the beetles become a problem. Use trap crops like radish mustard to attract them. Members of the cabbage family are the best trap crops. Use diamotecoeus earth or oils such as neem oil. These are effective organic controls. the application of insecticides containing carbaryl, spinosad, bifenthrin and permethrin.

Aphids (Peach aphid, Melon aphid)

Myzus persicae

Aphis gossypii

Symptoms

Aphids are small soft-bodied insects usually found on the underside of leaves and the stems of plants. The aphids are usually green or yellow. There are also pink, brown, red or black ones, depending on species and host plant. Heavy aphid infestation may cause the leaves to yellow and distort. Aphids secrete a sticky, sugary substance called honeydew. The honeydew encourages the growth of sooty mold on the plants.

Treatment

Simply rub the aphids off using thumb and forefinger in small infestations. Check transplants for aphids before planting them. Use insecticidal soaps or oils like neem or canola oil to control heavier infestations.

Cutworms

Agrotis spp.

Peridroma saucia

Nephelodes minians

Symptoms:

These caterpillars cut the stems of young plants off at the soil line. They can chew irregular holes into the surface of fruits. The larvae causing the damage is usually active at night. they hide during the day in the soil at the base of the plants or in plant debris. The larvae will usually curl up into a C-shape when disturbed. Squash them.

Treatment.

Cutworms have a wide host range and attack vegetables including asparagus, bean, cabbage family, carrot, celery, corn, lettuce, pea, pepper, potato and tomato. To control, remove all plant residue from soil after harvest or at least two weeks before spring planting. Use plastic or foil collars fitted around plant stems to cover the bottom three inches above the soil line and extending a couple of inches into the soil. Hand-pick the larvae after dark or spread diatomaceous earth around the base of the plants. Use appropriate insecticides to control the insects. Cutworms are more common in new garden plots, but can occur in older gardens.

Stinkbugs (Various)

Stinkbugs cause dark colored pinpricks on the fruit surrounded by a lighter area that turns yellow or remains light green. Stink bugs often carry diseases. The adult insect is shield-shaped and brown or green. They may have pink, red or yellow markings. The eggs are drum shaped and appear in clusters on the bottoms of the leaves. The larvae resemble the adults but are smaller. The adult insects survive over winter under leaves. They prefer legumes, blackberries or weeds such as mustard or Russian thistle.

Treatment:

Remove all weeds around garden that may protect the stink bugs. Keep weeds under control throughout the season. Insecticidal soaps, kaolin clay and neem oil may control them. There is a newer type of stink but that emerged around 2010 that is very hard to control.

Thrips (Western flower thrips, Onion thrips)

Frankliniella occidentalis

Thrips tabaci

Symptoms:

High thrips populations may damage and distort leaves. The leaves appear silvery. Black feces may cover the leaves. the insect is small and slender. A hand lens works best to view it. Adult thrips are pale yellow to light brown. The nymphs are smaller and lighter in color

Thrips transmit viruses such as tomato spotted wilt virus.

Treatment:

Avoid planting cucumbers next to onions, garlic where large numbers of thrips can accumulate. Use insecticides to control them.

Cucumber Green Mottle Mosaic (Code - CGMMV)

Symptoms:

Early symptoms on young plants include the development of crumpled leaves. Older plants may bleach out. As the infection progresses the leaves blister and distort. The leaf symptoms are difficult to distinguish from other mosaic viruses. Severity of symptoms varies depending on the strain of the virus. All cucurbit species like squash and melons are susceptible to the virus. Some cucumber varieties have some resistance to the disease.

Treatment:

Infected seed is the main cause of the disease. Use only disease-free seed from a reputable supplier. Remove all plants infected with the disease. Remove all the plants within a three to five food radius, as they may have it. The virus can be by tools and hands. Practice good sanitation to prevent virus transmission. Disinfect all tools and equipment between uses by dipping in a solution of bleach.

Verticulum wilt

Fungus - Verticillium dahliae

Symptoms

Symptoms generally appear after the fruits form. The symptoms include yellow leaves that develop dead areas. The leaves will collapse. The symptoms appear on only on one side of vine and there is discoloration of vascular tissue in roots. The fungus can survive in soil for many years. Cool or mild weather in spring encourages the disease.

Treatment:

Do not plant where other susceptible crops were grown the previous year. Delay planting until temperatures are warmer.

Alternaria leaf blight

Alternaria cucumerina

Symptoms

Small, yellow-brown spots with a yellow or green halo first appear on the oldest leaves. As the disease progresses the lesions expand and become large dead patches. These often have a concentric pattern. The lesions will coalesce and the leaves begin to curl and eventually die. The disease is prevalent in growing areas where temperatures are high and with frequent rain.

Management

Rotate all cucurbits with another crop every two years. Clean up crop debris after harvest. Alternatively till it deep into the soil. Use fungicides to slow the development of the disease. Irrigate the plants from the base rather than from above. Use drip irrigation.

Cercospora leaf spot

Fungus - Cercospora citrullina

Symptoms:

The first symptoms occur on older leaves as small spots with light to tan brown centers. As the disease progresses the lesions enlarge to cover large areas of the leaf. The lesions may have a dark border. The centers of the lesions may become brittle and crack easily. The fungus survives on plant debris. Wind and water splash from rain can spread the disease. It occurs mainly in tropical and subtropical growing regions.

Treatment:

Remove and destroy any diseased plants to prevent further spread. Remove and destroy any diseased plant material at the end of the season.

Septoria leaf spot

Fungus - Septoria cucurbitacearum

Symptoms:

The initial symptoms of the disease are small, dark water-soaked spots on the leaves. These spots turn beige to white in dry conditions. The lesions develop thin brown borders and the centers may become brittle and crack. Small white spots may erupt on the surface of infected butternut and acorn squash and pumpkin fruit. The pathogen can survive on crop debris for a year.

Treatment:

Scout plants during cool wet conditions for spots. Apply fungicide early to limit the development of the disease. Rotate cucurbits with other crops every two years.

Bacterial leaf spot

Bacterium - Xanthomonas campestris

Symptoms:

The disease first appears as small water-soaked lesions on the undersides of the leaves. These lead to yellow patches on the upper leaf surface. The lesions become round and may be mistaken for angular leaf spot. The centers of the lesions become thin and translucent. A wide yellow halo will surround the lesion. The bacteria spreads through infected seeds.

Treatment:

Use disease-free seed from a reputable seed supplier. Do not grow plants where cucurbits have been grown in the previous two years. Avoid overhead irrigation, water plants from the base to reduce the spread of bacteria or use trickle irrigation.

Aster yellows

Aster yellows phytoplasma

Symptoms:

The disease causes the Foliage to turn yellow. There will be an abnormal number of secondary shoots. The stems become rigid and with and upright growth habit. The leaves are often small and distorted. They may become thick. The; flowers are often disfigured and fruits small and pale. Leafhoppers carry the disease and can cause huge losses.

Treatment:

Remove infected plants to reduce spread. Control the weeds in and around the garden that may act as a habitat for the insects. Protect plants from leaf hoppers with row covers

Squash mosaic

Squash mosaic virus (Code - SqMV)

Symptoms:

Symptoms vary with variety, but plants can show symptoms that include mottled leaves, blisters, ring spots or protruding veins at leaf margins. Infected plants are often stunted and fruits may be malformed. The virus can be transmitted through infected seed and spread by striped cucumber beetles.

Treatment:

Use only certified disease-free seed from reputable seed suppliers.

Watermelon mosaic

Watermelon mosaic virus (Code - WMV)

Symptoms

Symptoms can vary widely depending on species. Symptoms on leaves may include green mosaic pattern, yellow rings and disfigured leaves. The virus is found in almost all cucurbit growing regions in the world. the virus is spread by over twenty aphid species

Treatment:

Controlling aphids can also control the virus. Spraying plants with mineral oils or insecticidal soaps can control aphids.

Medicinal uses:

The author does not recommend nor endorse use of daylily as a medicine or food. This section is for informational uses only. If you want to use this as an herb or for medical uses it is best to consult with a physician or health care provider before doing so.

Cucumber seeds can act as a diuretic to induce urination. The most common use was as a taeniacide to rid the body of tapeworms and other internal parasites. One or two ounces of seeds were ground and mixed with sugar and a bit of water to form a paste. People took this to cleanse the body of the parasite Cucumber juice finds use as a facial cleanser and to treat skin disorders. Commercial skin products still use cucumber juice as an ingredient. Native tribes in California roasted the seeds and ate them to cure kidney disorders.

Food Uses:

The fruit is the most commonly eaten product of the cucumber vine. Cooks add it to vegetable salads, or slice it to eat raw. The cucumber can be pickled or cooked. Pickling it is probably the most common use. Some people find the cucumber indigestible due to the cellulose content. The seed is also edible raw and has a nutty flavor. It contains an oil that is similar to olive oil. The oil contains 22.3% linoleic acid, 58.5% oleic acid, 6.8% palmitic acid and 3.7% stearic acid. Some like to cook, or steam, the young stems and leaves of the plant.

Harvesting:

Harvest cucumbers while the fruit is still young, before it starts to turn yellow. Once it starts yellowing, seeds have started to form. The seeds are bitter and the flesh begins to get bitter at this time. Picking the cucumber young encourages the vine to continue production.

Storage:

Cucumbers will not keep long, even in the refrigerator. Commercial cucumbers growers coat their cucumbers with wax, enhancing their storage time. Home gardeners can store cucumbers up to two, maybe three days before they become soft. To prevent moisture loss, wrap the cucumbers in food grade cellophane to prevent moisture loss. Thus wrapped, fresh cucumbers might keep up to seven or eight days. To store long term, you must pickle, freeze, dry or can them.

Types:

Gardeners will find four main types of cucumbers to grow in the garden. These are slicing, pickling, and burpless and Armenian cucumbers.

Slicing Cucumbers

Slicing cucumbers are the most common type found in the home garden and the produce case. Commercially grown slicing cucumbers have somewhat thicker skins than varieties commonly grown in the home garden. This is because the commercial cucumbers have to withstand shipping and handling. Those grown for the home garden or farmer's market have thinner skins, and in the opinion of many, a better taste. Slicing cucumbers are long, thin and eaten raw, sliced or in salads.

Pickling Cucumbers

Any cucumber is suitable for pickling. However, the types of cucumbers grown for pickling by commercial growers tend to be shorter and more irregular in shape. The skin is bumpier and the fruit is less uniform in shape and size. Many of the pickling cucumbers are available for home gardeners that want a smaller cucumber to pickle and can. These include the "gherkin" types.

Burpless Cucumbers

Burpless cucumbers have a thinner skin than regular cucumbers. Many find them sweeter and easier to digest. They have fewer seeds and can grow to almost two feet in length.

Armenian Cucumber

These are a different species, Cucumis melo var. flexuosus. They have a thin skin that does not require peeling to eat. The have long, thin, ribbed fruit that is actually more like a melon. These are sold in the Middle Eastern markets as "pickled wild cucumber."

Cooking and Preparing:

Most cucumbers are eaten raw, sliced or in salads. Since the skin can be bitter, most people skin them first, however the thinner-skinned varieties may be eaten without skinning them. Since most of the nutrition value is in the skin, this would be the best way to eat fresh cucumbers. Cucumbers can also be fried, sautéed and baked. They also find use in vegetable dips and soups. They can also be roasted in the oven for a tasty treat.

Drying Cucumbers

If the cucumbers have a thick skin, peel before drying. If they are a thin-skinned variety, just wash them well and slice into one-eighth inch slices. If they have gotten seedy, slice them lengthwise and scrape out the seeds, then cut them into slices. Lay them in a single layer on the dryer tray and salt, if desired. Dry at 125 degrees Fahrenheit for eight hours for crispy slices, six hours for chewy slices.

Freezing Cucumbers

It is possible to freeze cucumbers, though the conventional process of blanching and freezing common for most vegetables will not work well. To freeze cucumbers, the most used recipe is the brine method. Home grown or cucumbers purchased at a local farmers market work the best, but store bought cucumbers will also work. Since smaller cucumbers work the best, use cucumbers no more than four or five inches long and less than two inches in diameter. You can peel them, or not, depending on personal preferences. If using store bought cucumbers and you choose not to peel, remove the wax coating commercial growers use to preserve it by brushing the fruit with a vegetable brush under warm, running water.

Use this recipe for two quarts of sliced cucumbers. Adjust quantities as needed.

Slice the cucumbers into thin slices. Use a mandolin, paring knife or vegetable slicer. You may also add sliced onions to the cucumbers, if desired. The standard is to use one medium onion per two quarts of cucumbers. Layer the cucumbers and onions in a large bowl, adding about two tablespoons of salt between the layers. If using a bowl with a sealable lid, you may put the lid on and shake the mixture well to assure uniform mixture of the salt. Cover the bowl and allow to cure for at least two hours. Overnight is fine.

After curing, rinse the cucumber/onion mix in a colander, removing all the salt. Pour them back into the bowl, after rinsing it.

To make the brine, mix two-thirds cup of vinegar with one and a half cups of sugar. Pour this mix over the cucumbers and stir it well to mix the brine evenly throughout. Other spices like celery seed and garlic powder may be added now, if desired.

Spoon the cucumber mix into freezer containers or freezer bags. If using freezer containers or can/freeze jars, make sure to leave about a half inch of headspace to allow for expansion. Label the containers with the date and recipe used, if you are experimenting with different recipes. Leave for at least one week.

Thaw overnight in the refrigerator before use. Eat them as is for a crunchy treat, or chop them for use in sauces, relishes or other vegetable dish.

You may also juice or puree sliced cucumbers and freeze in ice cube trays. Use this frozen juice in smoothies. Frozen cucumbers should last about a year.

Canning and Pickling Cucumbers:

Pickling cucumbers is not hard, but it does call for a modest investment in equipment. Some of the equipment you may already have, others will find other uses in the kitchen. The items you will need include:

One large pot - Teflon lined, glass, stainless steel, glassware, enamelware or ceramic.

One Canning Pot

Pint canning jars Wide mouth is preferable. You can use quarts, if desired. Canning jars are reusable many times for many different vegetables.

Large spoons and ladles

Jar grabber for taking jars out of the hot canner

Canning Jar Lids - the lids are used only once, and then discard.

Jar Lid Rings -These are metal bands that secure the lids to the jars. You may use these many times.

Pickling Equipment notes:

The basic equipment used for pickling is similar to other types of canning. However, there are some differences:

Do not use utensils made of zinc, iron, brass, copper, or galvanized metal. These metals may react with the acids and salts and. This can cause undesirable color and taste changes in the pickles or make pickles inedible. Do not use enamelware with cracks or chips.

Lid lifter - these have a magnet on them for picking lids out of boiling water

Jar funnel - Use this wide mouthed funnel to pack vegetables in the jars.

Steps in Pickle Making

Use fresh picked cucumbers. The type of cucumber depends on the type of pickle you want to make. Small, pickling cucumbers works well to pickle whole as sweet or dill pickles. Use thin sliced cucumbers for bread and butter or dill slices. Wash the cucumbers and cut, slice or leave whole, as desired. It is best to cut the blossom end of the cucumber off. The blossom end is the end that will not have the small nubbin that shows where the vine attached to the fruit.

Commercial Pickling Mix

Most grocery stores sell ready-made pickling mixes. These mixes are available in many different flavors. To make these, follow the instructions on the packet. Here are some of the more popular mixes:

Mrs. Wages (http://store.mrswagesstore.com/pickles.html), Ball Pickling Products. (http://www.freshpreserving.com/products/pickling)

The steps below are only to outline the process. The pickle mixes may require different steps. Some of these mixes make a pickle that does not need canning. These are called "refrigerator pickles" and are outlined later in this book.

Before starting, it is best to sterilize the jars, lids and rings. Test the jars first, to make sure the rim has no crack or imperfections. Run your fingertip along the rim of each jar. If you feel a bump or other imperfection, the jar will probably not seal. Do not use that jar for canning. Fill the canner with water, leaving some room at the top. Submerge the jars in the water and bring this to a boil. Remove the jars from the water, empty and place upside down on the kitchen counter on a clean towel. Using a small pan, fill with water and put the jars and lids in the water. Boil the jars and rings for a few minutes and then take them out, lay on a towel beside the jars.

If you have a dishwasher that has a "sanitizer" cycle, using that will work fine. Then you will not have to boil the jars or lids.

After sterilizing the jars, prepare the brine. You can use your own mix if you have an old family recipe or other. There are literally hundreds of recipes available on the internet and each will have its own instructions. If you are a total beginner, the author recommends you start with a prepared mix. After you have the hang of it, feel free to experiment. Prepare the cucumbers and the brine as per the instructions on the packet.

Using the jar funnel, pack the cucumbers in the jar.

Fill the jars with the brine, leaving some headspace.

Place the lids on the jars and secure with the canning rings. Put the jars in the canner with at least one inch of water in the bottom. Boil, usually about ten minutes, but individual recipes will vary. Lift the jars out of the canner using the jar lifter. Place these on a towel or jar rack and allow to cool. After the jars begin cooling, you may hear a sharp, metallic "clink." This means the jars are sealing. When cool, use your finger to poke down in the center of the lid. If sealed properly, the lid will not move. If it allows you to press it down, it did not seal. Sometimes the jars do not seal because of a defect in the glass jars rim, sometimes there is a small piece of debris under the lid. Take the lids off and inspect the jar rims for defects or debris. There is no need to re-sterilize them if reprocessed quickly. Or, just put them in the refrigerator and use them right away.

Place the sealed jars in a cool place to store. Sealed canning jars will keep at least a year.

Note there are no ingredients or quantities listed, as all recipes will call for different things. Common ingredients include vinegar, dill, pickling spice, salt, celery seed and sugar. The packaged mixes will probably include everything but the vinegar.

Refrigerator Pickles

Refrigerator pickles, or quick pickles, are ready to eat in a few days and require no processing. The basic procedure is to put raw cucumbers or pickles into a jar with the spices you want to use. Boil the pickling solution and pour it over the pickles, filling to within one-half inch of the top. Allow this to cool, and then put the pickles in the refrigerator. These should keep for several weeks.

Here is one simple recipe.

Ingredients

1 1/3 cups white sugar

2 tablespoons salt

1 cup white vinegar

6 cups peeled and sliced cucumbers

2 cups sliced onion

Place the cucumbers in clean jars with the onions. Mix the solution and fill the jars. This one you do not need to boil. Put on the lids and refrigerate for two days. You may vary this recipe as desired, adding different ingredients like green peppers, pimentos, garlic and other goodies.

There are also several pre-mixed ingredient packets in the two product lines listed in the Canning Pickles sections. These will have instructions.

Fermented pickles

Using a salt brine to ferment and preserve pickles, as well as many other vegetables, is a time-honored way to put food aside for winter. The pioneers used this method to keep vegetables in an age before refrigeration. All you need to ferment pickles is salt, fresh cucumbers, and herb flavorings.

Prepare the brine using about one tablespoon of salt to one quart of water.

Wash the cucumbers. It is important to make sure the cucumbers are as fresh as possible to have crunchy cucumbers as the final product. Using cucumbers that are not fresh picked may result in a soggy cucumber.

Cut the cucumbers into slices, cubes or leave them whole.

Place the seasonings into the bottom of the canning jar, crock, glass or plastic bowl. Seasonings can include onion, garlic, dill, bay leaves, celery seed or others.

Put the cucumbers on top of the seasonings.

Pour the brine over the cucumbers, making sure that the cucumbers stay completely submerged.

Allow to ferment for at least one week. These should keep for several weeks, if prepared properly. If using canning jars with lids make sure, you remove them after a few days to allow fermentation gasses to escape. Refrigeration will allow them to last longer.

Nurseries Plants Available From

There are a number of online, mail order sources of supply for cucumber and other vegetable plants. It is best to purchase your cucumber plants from a local nursery. In the event there is no local source or you have no time to go to a nursery, here are some online sources.

Garden Harvest Supply

Local Calls: 260-589-3384

Toll Free Calls: 888-907-4769

Garden Harvest Supply

2952W 500S

Berne IN 46711

http://www.gardenharvestsupply.com/

Lowe's

http://www.lowes.com/Plants-Planters/Plants-Bulbs-Seeds/Vegetable-Plants

Bonnie Plants,

Kimberly Harruff

Bonnie Plants

1727 Hwy 223

Union Springs, Alabama 36089

http://bonnieplants.com/

Gurney's Seed & Nursery Co

Customer Service

P.O. Box 4178

Greendale, IN 47025-4178

Order Phone: 812-260-2153

Customer Service Phone: (513) 354-1492

http://www.gurneys.com/category/vegetables

W. Atlee Burpee & Co.

300 Park Avenue

Warminster, PA 18974

1 (800) 888-1447

http://www.burpee.com/vegetables/

The Home Depot

1-800-HOME-DEPOT

1-800-(466-3337)

http://www.homedepot.com/b/Outdoors-Garden-Center-
Garden-Plants-Flowers-Vegetable-Plants/N-5yc1vZc8r4

Park Seed Co.

3507 Cokesbury Road

Hodges, SC 29653

Phone Number: 1-800-845-3369

Monday - Friday 8AM - 6PM

Saturday 8AM - 5PM

Closed Sunday

Contact Email: info@parkseed.com

http://parkseed.com/

Note: this list is not all inclusive as there are many reputable companies offering vegetable seedlings and plants online. The author does not necessarily reccomend, nor recieve compensation from, any of these sources.

Nutrition:

Serving size: ½ cup (52g) fresh cucumber with peel

Amount Per Serving

Calories 10 Calories from Fat 0

% Daily Value*

Total Fat 0g 0%

 Saturated Fat 0g 0%

 Trans Fat 0g

Cholesterol 0mg 0%

Sodium 0mg 0%

Total Carbohydrate 2g 1%

 Dietary Fiber 0g 0%

Sugars 1g

Protein 0g

Vitamin A 2%

Vitamin C 2%

Calcium 0%

Iron 0%

Cultivars:

This list is not exhaustive. It should cover most of the varieties available to the home gardener. Check the seed catalog list at the end of this volume for our list of seed catalogs.

Greenhouse cucumbers

Bella Cucumbers

68 days.

Elongated, slender fruits with a crisp texture and the sweet, refreshing flavor of summer.

Rocky Cucumbers

46 days

The perfect one bite, seedless cucumber that is ideal for snacks, salads, and lunch boxes.

Telegraph Improved Cucumbers

60 days.

Telegraph improved is one of the most requested open-pollinated greenhouse varieties.

Manny Cucumbers Organic

52 days.

Crisp, shiny, spineless cukes that are specifically bred to thrive in the greenhouse during colder months .

Pickling cucumbers

Excelsior Cucumbers Organic

50 Days

Beautiful, emerald-green cukes have exquisite flavor — perfect for fresh eating or pickling.

Pickling Cucumbers

Boston Pickling Cucumber

This is an enormously productive old variety that will continue to bear throughout a long growing season if the fruits are gathered as soon as they are large enough to use. Fruits are smooth, bright green, about 5-1/2 inches long by 2-1/2 inches across, and blunt ended. Fruits seldom get too large for pickles.

Calypso Hybrid Pickler Cucumber

Calypso is a high yield combined with outstanding disease resistance. This one is recommended if your cucumbers are susceptible to cucumber mosaic, powdery mildew or bacterial wilt. Mid-green fruits are five inches long at maturity with no bitterness. Ideal for pickling and salads.

County Fair Hybrid Cucumber

County Fair is the only cucumber resistant to bacterial wilt. Nearly 100% female flowers allow it to set fruit without a pollinator. Almost seedless if kept isolated from other cucumbers. Sweet, non-bitter flavor and crunchy, firm texture makes it a good slicer. It is very productive with multiple disease resistance.

Fancy Pickling Type Cucumber

This is an exceptionally heavy bearer. Dark green, cylindrical fruits with blocky ends pack up perfectly in the jar. It is good for all types of pickles. Fruits average 6 to 7 in., but pick sweet pickles at 2 in. Black-spined. Huge yields. Disease resistant

H-19 Little Leaf Cucumber

This variety was developed by the university of Arkansas and may be the highest yielding pickling cucumber on the market today. Compact, vigorous vines set 20 to 30 bright green blocky fruits per plant at one time, the small 2" triangular leaves making it easy to find the fruit. It keeps on producing 3 to 5 weeks longer than most varieties. Tolerates heat, drought and cool temperatures, has resistance to many cucumber diseases, plus the ability to set fruit without bee pollination.

Homemade Pickles Cucumber

Homemade pickles is for anyone who likes to harvest lots of cucumbers for their favorite pickle recipes. This disease resistant, vigorous grower bears exceptionally high yields of uniform medium green fruits with small white spines. Harvest them when small for tiny sweets, at 5 to 6 inches for robust dills and spears, or any size in between. The interior flesh is solid and crisp, just right for delicious crunchy pickles.

Pick A Bushel Hybrid Cucumber

This one is ideal for baby pickles. It feathers heavy yields of petite fruits about 1 inch by 3-1/2 inches with medium to small seed cavities, mild flavor and crisp texture. Vigorous vines adapt well to most soils, even heavy clay types. It exhibits some resistance to downy and powdery mildew. 34 Days.

Bush Pickle Cucumbers

45-50 days.

A mini plant with major production. Bush pickle bends the cucumber rules by not vining out.

Wautoma Cucumbers

60 days

This is an early, very productive pickling cucumbe.

Homemade Pickles Cucumbers

60 days

The vigorous 5 foot vines exhibit excellent disease resistance, and yield armloads of solid, crisp cucumbers.

Double Yield Cucumbers Organic

52 days

There couldn't be a more appropriate name for this industrious cucumber. Its productivity is unmatched.

Alibi Cucumbers

50 days

Poised to meet your pickling needs at its mature 3-4 inch length, this early cucumber can be picked even when longer.

Mcpick Cucumbers

65 days

This is the crunchiest pickling cucumber with deep green, sleek skin and buff-colored spines.

Diamant Cucumbers

47 days

This is an early gherkin with outstanding, uniform pickling cucumbers.

Slicing Cucumbers

Armenian Yard Long Cucumber

This burpless and bitterfree cucumber will grow to two to three feet long. These light green ribbed delicacies are best eaten when about 12 to 15 inches long. Fruits set well at high temperatures and are straighter when grown on a fence or a trellis.

Burpless Hybrid Cucumber

Tasty green and low in acid makes for easy digestion. Extremely mild and practically acid-free, so you can eat all you want. Slender fruits about 10 to 12 in. Long. It has no bitter taste. Fruits look best - long and straight - when grown on a trellis. Otherwise they may grow curved. Looks like breadstick cucumbers.

Diva Cucumber

There are sweet, crisp fruits on this high-yielding slicing cucumber. Its glossy bright green skins are spineless and very tender, particularly when harvested at 4 to 6 inches. The all-female flowers don't require pollen to set fruit, so yields are higher and fruits are nearly seedless. The five to six foot vines bear at nearly every node and non-bitter foliage is unattractive to cucumber beetles. Resists scab and has tolerance to powdery and downy mildews.

Improved Long Green Cucumber

The largest main season variety we offer. Fruits are extra-long, dark green, slender, tender and free from bitterness. Twelve inches long by three inches across at maturity. It has an enormous yield of slices. Black spines. Flesh is white, very crisp and good flavored.

Longfellow cucumber

This one has extremely long, twelve to fifteen inch length, slender and round-ended. Fruits dotted with white spines, are a uniform dark green. Flesh is firm, of excellent quality, with few seeds. It is perfect for slicing.

Marketer Cucumber

Marketer is a heat tolerant eight inch slicing salad cucumber. With its vigorous, high yielding plants, this heirloom cucumber produces mild tasting fruits for great salads and delicious pickle chips.

Marketmore 76 Cucumber

The best combination of attractiveness and disease resistance. Fruits are crisp, long and straight, up to nine inch long with beautiful, dark green skin. Fruit holds attractive color in summer heat. It is ideal for disease-prone gardens. It is resistant to scab and mosaic virus. Vines bear over a long period.

Pick A Bushel Hybrid Cucumber

This is a high yielder of three to six inch, white spined cucumbers. Sweet, crispy fruits are perfect for pickling, as well as eating fresh. Semi-bush plants are excellent for small gardens, patio containers and are heat tolerant with good disease resistance.

Poinsett 76 Cucumber

This one is ideal for the south. It is resistant to leaf spot, anthracnose, scab, downy mildew and powdery mildew. Very dark green fruits are best at eight inches long. Very good yields and highly reliable.

Straight Eight Cucumber

This is an extremely popular early variety. It is an All-America winner. It has perfectly straight, dark green fruits about eight inches long with a small seed cavity. It is excellent for slicing, salads or dills. White spines.

58 Days

Sweet Slice Hybrid Cucumber

This one tastes sweet like sugar, with no bitterness. Major breeding triumph now permits sweetness with no "burp" or bitterness on one plant. Vigorous vines have excellent yields. Highly disease resistant plants. Fruits are slim, long at ten to twelve inches and tapered, slightly curved and medium dark green. It needs no peeling. White spined.

Sweet Success Hybrid Cucumber

This is the ultimate 'burpless' cucumber for growing inside or outdoors. It produces loads of long, straight spineless fruits twelve to fourteen inches long by three inches in diameter. Sweet, mild flesh is seedless if grown away from other cucumbers. It sets quality fruit without pollen. It has good disease resistance. To grow fruits with no seeds, keep in a greenhouse where it cannot be pollinated.

61 days

Sweeter Yet Hybrid Cucumber

This is the ultimate burp-free cucumber. Sweeter yet takes the flavor, quality and early maturity of burpless cucumbers to a new level. The sweet flavor is at its peak when the cylindrical fruits are harvested at 10 to 12 inches long. The dark green thin skin is non-bitter and need not be peeled away. Vigorous, disease-resistant seventy to eight inch vines can be grown trellised or allowed to spread on the ground. Enjoy exceptional yields from this gynecocious hybrid. pollen.

Height: 0"

width: 0"

spacing: 0"

48 Days

Tendergreen Burpless Cucumber

This Eighty-year- variety is easy on the digestion and the pocketbook! About six inches long by two inches across, slightly blocky, light green in color, with white spines. Tender, extra-sweet flesh is ideal for slicing or pickling. It has good disease resistance.

55 Days

Summer Dance Cucumbers

65 days

Crisp, clean, flavor.

Marketmore 97 cucumbers

55 days

Developed at Cornell University, Marketmore 97 is a great slicing cucumber, and is one of the most disease-resistant.

Raider cucumbers

52 days

A champion performer in the garden and unquestionable producer of tasty, crisp, and delicious cucumbers.

Pepinex cucumbers

65-70 days

Flawless and refined, Pepinex produces premium English-type cucumbers on productive plants.

Rocky Cucumbers

46 days

The perfect one bite, seedless cucumber that is ideal for snacks, salads, and lunch boxes.

Armenian Cucumbers

c. Melo

60 days

Called snake melons in the middle east, this cucumber relative develops slightly ribbed fruits.

Patio Snacker Cucumbers

50-55 days

Whether you are tight for space or just want a terrific container cuke, this one's for you.

General Lee Cucumbers

66 days

General Lee has vigorous, robust, healthy plants, and huge yields.

Boothbys Blonde Cucumbers

60-65 days

This small and uniquely attractive cucumber is an heirloom variety from the Boothby family in Livermore.

Slicing Cucumbers

Fountain Cucumbers

65 days

This is an all-around exceptional slicing cucumber.

Lime Crisp Cucumbers

60 days

This cucumber has crisp, crunchy, and refreshing with a unique, light green skin.

Alibi cucumber

This is a true miniature cucumber. Fruits are three to four inches long, but can be harvested at 2 inches for smooth gherkin pickles. If you keep them picked, they'll produce all season. Vigorous, small plants.

Beit Alpha Cucumber

(F1 Hybrid 52 Days)

Also called a lebanese or middle eastern cucumber, much of the breeding work on these varieties has been done in israel. The large, smooth, somewhat blocky, burpless, and nearly spineless fruit can be either pickled or eaten fresh. The flavor, including that of the skin, is very mild. 25 Seeds. Learn more

Bush Crop Cucumber

(55 days)

This slicing type combines a full size six to eight inch cucumber with a short, two to three foot bushy plant and no runners. It forms a neat, attractive mound. Fruit are quite crispy and juicy with good flavor.

Crystal Apple Cucumber

This is a prolific variety first introduced from New Zealand in 1934. It has its best flavor in its young stage at about two inches with tender pale greenish skin and mildly sweet flesh. A great little novelty cucumber to show off to your friends plus it compliments a salad well.

Delikatesse Cucumber

(60 days) (heirloom)

This German heirloom is a popular European variety and a bit different from US cucumber in appearance. Fruits are about ten inches long with a lovely pale, almost lime-green color, and covered with tiny warts. It can be used as a fine slicer or a very large pickler. The abundant yields are one reason that Delikatesse has stood the test of time, great flavor is the other.

Diva Cucumber

(58 days)

Diva is a nearly seedless parthenocarpic variety. It produces exclusively female flowers that do not require pollination to set fruit. Diva is considered a beit alpha type, the smooth skinned class of fruits that originated in the middle east. Fruits are very crisp with an attractive medium green color and very sweet, never bitter flavor. Diva is resistant to scab and mildews.

Burpless Cucumbers

Garden Sweet Burpless Cucumber

(f1 hybrid 60 days)

Mild flavored as the name implies, these eleven inch, disease resistant cucumbers are great for either pickling or eating fresh. Vines are vigorous climbers and yields are heavy. The skin is very smooth and of course, the flesh is not bitter. A hybrid of the Japanese long cuke. 25 Seeds.

H-19 Little Leaf Cucumber

(57 days)

This one is great for slicing or pickling. This reliable variety has multi branching compact vines, small foliage for ease of picking and needs no pollination, making it a good choice for protecting against insects when growing under row cover. Utilize this cuke in the garden, containers or greenhouse. It yields even under stress and has some resistance to mosaic virus, downy and powdery mildew.

Heike Cucumber

(f1 hybrid, 58 days)

This one produces predominantly female flowers for earlier harvests and large yields. Slender, dark green fruit is bitter free and matures to twelve to thirteen inches, Grow under tunnels and cold frames or in the open field.

Homemade Pickles Cucumber

(54 days)

The ideal size and shape of these cucumbers as well as the crisp texture and good flavor make it the quintessential pickling cucumber. Whether picked small for tiny gherkins, medium size for dill spears, or large for bread and butter slices, the medium green, short, plump cucumbers are perfect. The three foot vines are vigorous and prolific, ensuring that you have plenty of the best ever homemade pickles.

Little Tyke Cucumber

(35 days)

This is a great, prolific pickling cucumber. During harvest time each plant brings forth petite, tender fruits that grow great in hot climates and have a good keeping quality. Little Tyke has primarily female flowers so it is best planted along with another early cucumber

Long Green Improved Cucumber

(70 days) (Heirloom)

This is a black spine type, growing twelve to thirteen inches long and three inches in diameter. It is very popular for slicing and salting when mature, and when small, much esteemed for pickling.

Mexican Sour Gherkin Cucumber

(75 days)

Diminutive, watermelon looking fruits have a cucumber like taste with a lemony-lime burst. Easy to grow, having rampant vines, best grown on a trellis or in hanging baskets and easily ignored by pests. Harvest when they are smaller than a grape; the bigger they get the more sour citrus flavor they get. Eat them raw as a snack and in salads or preserve by pickling. Native to Central America and also known as mouse melon, sandita, cucamelon.

Miniature White Cucumber

(49 days)

This small white pickling cucumber is a heavy yielder. The oval cucumbers have a thin skin and the flavor is quite sweet. This black spined variety is never bitter.

Muncher Cucumber

(54 days)

While the vines are compact, they are also very strong, making Muncher a fine choice for container growing. It is a middle eastern - beit alpha type so the skin is very smooth and practically spineless. Delicious, burpless, and never bitter, the heavy yields of Muncher also pickles well at about the four inch size. It will reach nine inch at full maturity.

National Pickling Cucumber

(52 days)

This old standby provides a nice combination of earliness and abundant yields. Fruit can be used at any size, growing to be six inches long, three inches wide, and a dark mottled green. Vines are rambling and prolific.

Painted Serpent Cucumber

The fruits are light green with darker striped ribs that curl into snakelike shapes. It grows three to four feet long, but best picked at fifteen inches. It produces on a long vine. The mild, delicious fruit are not a true cucumber but a melon. Originated in Armenia.

Parisian Pickle Cucumber

(50 Days) (Heirloom)

This is an improved Bourbonne type. It used extensively in the commercial production of both Cornichons and gherkins in the late 19th century. Fruits are longer and thinner than pickling cucumbers in this country but well covered with little bumps (spines). It can grow to six inches with a slight curve on lengthy vines. It is also a fine slicer.

Picolino Cucumber

This is a miniature English cucumber with tender, thin skin, a crisp, crunchy and sweet taste. All from 4 inch fruits that can be grown in the garden or a greenhouse. It will be hard not to eat all these little guys straight from the vine but with the high yields from the all-female flowers (parthenocarpic, fruits set without pollination) you will be inundated. Keep picking continuously for a long harvest. Not the cheapest seed around but we love these cukes so much we wanted to offer them to our customer who might want to splurge on one vegetable variety and try something new. Disease resistance: cucumber mosiac virus, cucumber vein yellows virus, powdery mildew, scab, target leaf spot.

Poona Keera Cucumber

(53 day heirloom)

This is white cucumber from India eventually turns a russet brown, can be eaten at any stage, and will always be crisp and sweet. The best thing about poona keera is that it is never, ever bitter.

Spacemaster Cucumber

(59 days)

This is a full sized eight inch cucumber, primarily a slicer, on a short 3 foot vine; good for trellising in a tight spot or in a container. Its nice flavor and appearance is enhanced by its resistance to mosaic and scab.

Summer dance cucumber

Thiss elongated Japanese type cucumber is notable in that every one of the fruit seem perfect. It is ten inches long, an inch wide with a deep green color and smooth skin. The plant is a very vigorous grower setting many lateral vines for high productivity. It is resistant to both powdery and downy mildew. The flavor is sweet, mild, and refreshing, no need to peel these.

Suyo Cucumber

(65 days)

Fourteen inch long oriental, "burpless" cucumber. Fruit is two inches in diameter and deeply grooved. Growing up a trellis will produce a large number of straight cucumbers though some will curve and twist in the most amazing way. It has a nice, sweet flavor.

Sweet Success Cucumber

The six foot vine is very vigorous and could use some support. Fruit is set without pollination (parthenocarpy) and thus is seedless like a greenhouse cucumber but this variety can be grown outside, in the presence of insects. Fruit is fourteen inches long and delicious.

Swing Cucumber

(f1 hybrid, 65 days)

A great cucumber with all female flowers for outdoor or greenhouse growing. Crisp, eight to ten inch fruit are slightly spined with a non bitter taste. Grows well in unfavorable weather elements and has a strong resistance to powdery mildew and scab.

West India Gherkin Cucumber

(65 days) (heirloom)

Heirloom 1793, this variety has been sold in the US since the early 1800's, we suspect it will appear quite unique to most home gardeners. The leaves don't resemble cucumber leaves at all; they look like watermelon leaves. Vines are long and bear multitudes of small oval fruit that are exceptionally spiny. Used for unusual and good tasting pickles, they will also add a bit of surprise to a salad.

White Wonder Cucumber

(60 days heirloom)

Heirloom pre 1890. this is an attractive white cucumber that originated in upstate New York. Black spined fruits are oval, six to nine inches long and the skin is ivory white when fruit are young, becoming more of a cream color at full maturity. The crisp flesh is mild tasting and delicious. This is a very productive, vigorous variety. 25 Seeds.

Bush Cucumbers

Bush Pickle Cucumber

The compact vines produce loads of three to four inch cucumbers. It is ideal for small gardens. They make tasty, crispy, whole pickles. Fruits will not get too big before you pick them.

Muncher Cucumber

A very tender variety that is excellent for fresh eating right out of the garden. Nearly spineless fruits are six to eight inches long and three inches wide on strong vigorous vines. Non-bitter, burpless cucumbers, can be eaten at any stage of growth. For pickles, fuits should be picked when four to six inches long.

65 Days

White Wonder Cucumber

An heirloom that produces fruits that are ivory white in color from the time they begin to form until they mature. They are excellent for slicing or as a pickler. Skin is smooth and very thin. Fruits grow to a nice size, about 7 in. Long by 3 in. Wide, and have rounded ends. Flesh is solid and crisp, with excellent eating quality. White spine

58 Days

Seed Catalog List

Amanda's Garden Native Perennial Nursery

Phone: 585-669-2275

amandasgarden@frontiernet.net

8410 Harper's Ferry Road

Springwater, NY 14560

http://www.amandasnativeplants.com/

Ambergate Gardens

8730 County Road 43,

Chaska, MN 55318-9358.

(877) 211-9769. $2

http://www.ambergategardens.com/index.html

Antonelli Brothers

407 Hecker Pass

Watsonville, CA 95076

Phone: 1-888-423-4664

Website: www.antonellibegonias.com

Email Contact: linda@antonellibegonias.com

Their specialty is the tuberous begonia, but they offer other plants too.

Bluestone Perennials, Inc.

7211 Middle Ridge Rd

Madison, OH 44057

1.800.852.5243

http://www.bluestoneperennials.com/

(800) 852-5243

Burgess Seed and Plant Co.

905 Four Seasons Road

Bloomington IL 61701

309-662-7761

www.eburgess.com

56 pages

Burgess offers an interesting mix of perennials, shrubs, trees, and vegetable seeds. There are also fruit and nut trees, roses, and strawberries.

Burpee

W. Atlee Burpee Company

Warminster PA 18974

1-800-888-1447

www.burpee.com

The W. Atlee Burpee Company is one of the leading seed companies

in the gardening industry. The catalog lists good selections of annual and perennial flowers as well as vegetable seeds. Many, many tomatoes listed in addition to sweet corn and squash.

Charley's Greenhouse

17979 State Road 536

Mount Vernon WA 98273-3269

1-800-322-4707

www.charleysgreenhouse.com

88 pages

If you love greenhouses, you will love this catalog. It has greenhouses of all types. Lean-to greenhouses, free standing one, small, portable greenhouses and large ones suitable for a small commercial grower. The catalog lists just about everything you need to grow plants, even if you don't have a greenhouse. Seed starter supplies, sprayers, irrigation equipment, composters, shredders, its all here.

CherryGal

Toll-Free: 888-752-0022

email: CherryGal@nc.rr.com

http://www.cherrygal.com/

Creek Hill Nursery

17 West Main Street

Leola, PA 17540

PH: 717-556-0000

Toll Free: 888-565-0050

http://www.creekhillnursery.com/

Dayton Nurseries, Inc.

3459 Cleveland-Massillon Rd.

Norton, OH 44203

330-825-3320

1-866-500-6605

http://www.daytonnursery.com/

Edmunds Roses

335 S High Street

Randolph, Wisconsin 53956

1-800-347-7609

www.edmundsroses.com

48 pages

45 pages of roses. Tea roses, miniature roses, old fashioned roses, just about any kind of rose you can think of. The last 3 pages are devoted to fertilizers, tools and insecticides you will need for your roses.

Everwilde Farms

Everwilde Farms, Inc.

PO Box 40

Sand Creek, WI 54765

Toll Free: 1 (888) 848-3837

Local: 1 (715) 658-0001

http://www.everwilde.com/

Farmers Seed and Nursery

Division of Plantron, Inc

818 NW 4th Street

Fairbault, MN 55021

1-850-7334-1623

www.farmerseed.com

40 pages

This catalog has a good selection of nursery stock including ornamental shrubs and trees. Fruit includes strawberries, blackberries and raspberries. Other types of fruit trees and vines, too. Nut trees, perennial plants and roses, also. There is a good selection of vegetable seed.

Farmtek

1440 Field of Dreams

Dyersville, IA 52040

1-800-327-6835

www.farmtek.com

Extensive offerings of greenhouse supplies, including conduit to use to build your own. It also has tarps, fencing, weather shield canopies of many types, lighting, fans and heating supplies. This is a general farm supply catalog with items of some interest to the gardener, as there are large greenhouses and smaller portable structures as well as gardening supplies.

Fleming's Flower Fields

 Lincoln, Nebraska

1-855-442-4488

1-559-920-1476

http://www.flemingsflowers.com/

Forest Farm

990 Tetherow Rd.

Williams, OR 97544-9599.

(541) 846-7269. $4

Phone Orders: (541)846-7269

Monday-Friday (8-4 PST)

Fax Orders: (541)846-6963

Email: plants@forestfarm.com

http://www.forestfarm.com/contact_us.php

Four Seasons Nursery

1706 Morrissey

Bloomington, IL 61704

www.4seasonsnurseries.com

48 pages

This catalog encompasses nursery plants of all types. Shrubs, perennials, and trees are included within its pages. Dwarf citris trees for the patio. It also includes fruit trees and berry plants.

Garden Crossings L.L.C.

4902 96th Ave.

Zeeland, MI 49464

Phone: (616) 875-6355

http://www.gardencrossings.com/

Gardeners Supply

128 Intervale Road

Burlington, VT 05401

1-800-427-3363

www.gardeners.com

This catalog focuses on organic gardening supplies. They have a wonderful selection of tomato towers. There are also containers for patio gardening, trelleses, kits to build raised beds and much more in this delightful catalog. There are many items suitalble as gifts for gardeners. You will also find growing supplies, seed starting supplies, fertilizers, organic pesticides and other gardening supplies.

George W. Park Seed Company

1 Parkton Ave

Greenwood, SC 29647-0001

1-800-845-3369

www.parkseed.com

146 pages

This bountiful catalog has extensive offerings of all categories of seeds - herbs, vegetables, annual and perennial seeds. There is also a generous offering of fruit and berry plants like grapes, blackberries and strawberries.

Gilbert H. Wild

PO Box 338

Sarcoxie, MI 64862-0338

1-888-449-4537

www.gilberthwild.com

This grower has been in business since 1885. The catalog offers a large selection of daylilies, iris and peonies. They do have many other perennials.

Great Garden Plants, Inc.

P.O. Box 1511

Holland, MI 49422-1511

http://www.greatgardenplants.com/

Greenwood Nursery

636 Myers Cove Road

McMinnville, TN 37110

1-800-426-0958

http://www.greenwoodnursery.com/

Grower's Supply

1440 Field of Dreams Way

Dyersville, IA 52040

1-800-476-9715

www.growerssupply.com

This is the ultimate greenhouse supply catalog, supplying everything from large commercial greenhouses to small, hobby houses. There are also cold frames, hot beds, raised bed kits for gardens, arched bridges, fencing and netting. Greenhouse heaters, benches, growing supplies, chemicals and all other greenhouse growing supplies.

Gurney's Seed and Nursery

PO Box 4178

Greendale, IN 47025-4178

513-354-1491

www.gurneys.com

66 Pages

Gurney's large format catalog offers large selections of vegetables, flowers, fruits and supplies for gardening. They also list trees, shrubs, roses, and nut trees. This is one of the older seed companies, they have been selling seeds for many years.

Harris Seeds

355 Paul Road

PO Box 24966

Rochester, NY 14624-0966

1-800-514-4441

www.harrisseeds.com

82 pages

Heavy selection of vegetable seeds, with a nice offering of flower seeds, too. They have almost 20 pages of gardening supplies like seed starting equipment, flats and carts.

Hidden Valley Nature Arts

36175 Alamar Mesa Drive

Hemet, California 92545

Phone: 951-926-7330

http://www.hiddenvalleyhibiscus.com/

High Country Gardens

2902 Rufina Street

Santa Fe, NM 87507-2929

Phone: 800-925-9387

Fax: 800-925-0097

Annuals

Bulbs

Perennials

Exotic Plants and Flowers

Flower, Vegetable and Wildflower Seeds

Garden Supplies, Tools and Power Equipment

Gifts and Decorative Accessories

Ground Covers, Shrubs, Trees, and Vines

Fertilizer, Weed & Pest Control Products

Magazines and Books

Ornamental Grasses and Plants

Roses

Other

High Country Gardens specializes in waterwise ("xeric") perennials and other plants that need very little or no extra water once established. With the widespread awareness of green, environmentally conscious practices, the use of drought tolerant plants has now spread from the high desert gardens of the Southwest to the entire nation. We have spent years offering and developing unusual garden-tested perennials, bulbs, cacti, succulents, grasses, and shrubs that ship right from our greenhouses to your landscape. The fragrant and colorful blossoms and foliage on many of our flowering xeriscape plants, such as Lavender, Penstemon, and Agastache, attract hummingbirds and butterflies.

Website: www.highcountrygardens.com

Click Here to Subscribe to our Newsletter

Email Contact: plants@highcountrygardens.com

HPS - Horticultural Products and Services

334 West Stroud Street

Randolph WI 53956

130 pages

1-800-322-7288

www.hpsseed.com

This catalog caters to the commercial market or greenhouse grower, though the gardener who grows larger quantities of plants may find it useful, too.

Flower plugs, seeds for flowers and vegetables, and grower supplies. The flower seeds include both annual and perennial. Most are available in both large, commercial quantities and smaller amounts suitable for the home grower. Grower supplies include seed starter units, flats and inserts, greenhouse supplies, fertilizers and insecticides.

John Scheepers Kitchen Garden Seeds

23 Tulip Drive

PO Box 838

Bantam, CT 06750-0638

1-860-567-6086

www.kitchengardenseeds.com

This catalog focuses on vegetables and herbs. It has unusual and old time varieties as well as some of the favorites. The salad green selection of seeds is excellent. There are also Asian greens and sprouting seeds. There are some flower seeds, mostly annual fragrant and cutting flowers. This is a nice catalog with some unusual seed offerings.

Johnny's Selected Seeds

955 Benton Ave.

Winslow, ME 04901

Phone: 877-564-6697

Fax: 800-738-6314

Annuals

Bulbs

Perennials

Flower, Vegetable and Wildflower Seeds

Fruit Trees and Berries

Garden Supplies, Tools and Power Equipment

Gifts and Decorative Accessories

Greenhouses and Indoor Gardening Supplies

Ground Covers, Shrubs, Trees, and Vines

Herbs and Vegetables

Irrigation Supplies and Equipment

Fertilizer, Weed & Pest Control Products

Magazines and Books

Ornamental Grasses and Plants

Johnny's Selected Seeds is a mail-order seed producer and merchant located in Albion and Winslow, Maine, USA. The company was established in 1973 by our Founder and Chairman Rob Johnston, Jr. Johnny's prides itself on its superior product, research, technical information, and service for home gardeners and commercial growers.

Our products include vegetable seeds, medicinal and culinary herb seeds, and flower seeds. We also offer unique, high quality gardening tools and supplies. Our Export Department ships seeds internationally, and welcomes your inquiry. Of course, we also ship throughout the United States. We sell both retail and wholesale, small to large quantities.

Website: Johnnyseeds.com

Click Here to Subscribe to our Newsletter

Email Contact: homegarden@johnnyseeds.com

J. W. Jung Seed Company

335 South High Street

Randolph, WI 53957-0001

1-800-247-5864

www.jungseed.com

115 Pages

Jung sells a very interesting mix of fruit trees and plants, shrubs and

trees, vegetable and flower seed, and gardening supplies. Perennial plants,

flower bulbs, lilies and roses are included in the offerings. This is a

"must have" catalog for the gardener.

Kelley Nurseries

Division of Plantron

410 8th Ave NW

Faribault, MN 55021

www.kelleynurseries.com

56 pages

This is strictly a nursery catalog with good selections of perennials, ground covers, roses,

and ornamental grasses. Sections of water plants and nut trees also listed. Strong sections of ornamental trees, shrubs and fruit plants.

VanBourgondien

PO Box 2000

Virginia Beach, VA 23450

1-800-622-9959

www.dutchbulbs.com

68 pages.

This catalog is full of plant bulbs and perennial plants. They have a very large selection of dahlias. Also tropical bulbs, cannas, peonies, daylilies, and lilies. The perennial selection is excellent.

Magnolia Gardens

1980 Bowler Road

Waller, TX 77484

936-931-9927

http://magnoliagardensnursery.com/

Michigan Bulb Company

Customer Service

P.O. Box 4180

Lawrenceburg, IN 47025-4180

Phone: (812) 260-2148

http://www.michiganbulb.com/

McClure & Zimmerman

335 South High Street

Randolph, WI 53956

1-800-883-6998

www.mzbulb.com

32 pages

Two catalogs per year, a spring one with the spring bulb offerings and a second one in the autumn for the fall selections.

Spring offerings include begonias, caladiums, cannas, daylilies, iris, and much more. Very large selection of bulbs and tubers.

Musser Forests

Dept S-07M

1880 Route 119 Highway N

Indiana PA 15701-7341

1-800-643-8319

www.musserforest.com

48 Pages

This is a nursery catalog for the landowner or nursery owner. The offerings are trees and shrubs, mostly in smaller sizes suitable for planting in nursery rows or containers. Some are suitable for planting in the garden. Most are offered in larger quantities of 5, 10, or more. Selections include evergreen trees, deciduous trees, shrubs, groundcovers, and perennial plants.

Nature Hills Nursery, Inc.

3334 North 88th Plaza

Omaha, NE 68134

Phone: 888-864-7663

Fax: 866-550-9556

Annuals

Bulbs

Perennials

Exotic Plants and Flowers

Flower, Vegetable and Wildflower Seeds

Fruit Trees and Berries

Garden Supplies, Tools and Power Equipment

Gifts and Decorative Accessories

Greenhouses and Indoor Gardening Supplies

Ground Covers, Shrubs, Trees, and Vines

Herbs and Vegetables

Irrigation Supplies and Equipment

Fertilizer, Weed & Pest Control Products

Magazines and Books

Ornamental Grasses and Plants

Roses

Other

Nature Hills Nursery, Inc. was originally founded in 2001 as a conifer and deciduous tree nursery. Nature Hills Nursery started as a local tree nursery serving a limited geographic area. Our company has evolved and responded to our customers' demand of quality nursery products. We continue to improve our on-line capabilities and expand our product offerings.

Website: www.naturehills.com

Email Contact: info@NatureHills.com

Niche Gardens

1111 Dawson Rd

Chapel Hill, NC 27516

(919) 967-0078.

http://www.nichegardens.com/

North Creek Nurseries - Corporate Office

388 North Creek Road

Landenberg, PA 19350

Tel.: 610-255-0100

Toll Free: 877-ECO-PLUG

http://www.northcreeknurseries.com/

Oakland Nurseries

http://oaklandnursery.com/

The Garden Centers below are affiliated with Oakland Nurseries

Columbus Garden Center

1156 Oakland Park Avenue

Columbus, OH 43224-3317

Phone: 614-268-3511

Fax: 614-784-7700

Delaware Garden Center

25 Kilbourne Road

Delaware, OH 43015

Phone: 740-548-6633

Fax: 740-363-2091

Dublin Garden Center

4261 West Dublin-Granville Road

Dublin, Ohio 43017

Phone: 614-874-2400

Fax: 614-874-2420

New Albany Garden Center

5211 Johnstown Road

New Albany, Ohio 43054

Phone: 614-917-1020

Fax: 614-917-1023

Outsidepride.com, Inc.

915 N. Main

Independence, OR 97351

800-670-4192

http://www.outsidepride.com/

Perennial Pleasures Nursery

P.O. Box 147

E. Hardwick

VT 05836.

(802) 472-5104. $3

http://perennialpleasures.net/

Perryhill Nurseries Ltd

Edenbridge Road

Hartfield

East Sussex

TN7 4JP

Phone:01892 770377

Fax: 01892 770929

Email: sales@perryhillNurseries.co.uk

http://www.perryhillnurseries.co.uk/locate/

Pinetree Garden Seeds

PO Box 300

New Gloucester, ME 04260

1-926-3400

www.superseeds.com

115 pages

The catalog claims over 900 varieties of seeds, bulbs, tubers, garden books and products. The listings are pretty extensive with the emphasis on vegetable seeds. There are sections for ethnic vegetables like Asian, Italian, and Latin American. The flower offerings include both annual and perennial flower seeds.

Plant Delights Nursery, Inc.

9241 Sauls Road

Raleigh, NC 27603

Phone: 919.772.4794

http://www.plantdelights.com/

Prairie Moon Nursery

32115 Prairie Lane

Winona, MN 55987

Toll Free: (866) 417-8156

http://www.prairiemoon.com

Restoration Seeds

1133 Old Highway 99 S.

Ashland, OR 97520

1-541-201-2688

http://www.restorationseeds.com/

Roots and Rhizomes

PO Box 9

Randolph, WI 53956-0009

1-800-374-5035

www.rootsrhizomes.com

60 pages

Specializing in choice daylilies, siberian iris, hostas, and perennials. If you like any of those plants, this beautiful catalog will have something you want. Twenty pages of daylilies are at the beginning of the catalog and they are followed by hostas, iris and much more. They also have a large selection of other perennials like astilbe, aster, coriopsis, and geraniums.

Seeds of Change

PO Box 15700

Santa Fe NM 87592-1500

1-888-762-7333

www.seedsofchange.com

This catalog is for vegetable lovers as it is mostly devoted to them, and all seeds sold by this company are certified organic. There is a section of flower seeds, but veggies take center stage. There is a full

page of garlic varieties! Gourmet greens and herbs are in good supply, too.

There is also a good selection of gardening books and gardening supplies.

Select Seeds

180 Stickney Hill Road

Union, CT 06076

1-860-684-9310

www.selectseeds.com

67 Pages

If you are looking for something a bit out of the mainstream or "different" then Select Seeds is the catalog you are looking for. Most of the seeds and plants offered are not found in the major outlets. Special sections for fragrant and old-fashioned plants are featured. This catalog is a must for the home gardener looking for a flower garden that stands out a bit.

Seymours Selected Seeds

334 West Stroud Street

Randolph, WI 53596

1-800-353-9516

www.seymourseedusa.com

46 pages

This small catalog is packed with a full selection of annual and

perennial flowers for the home gardner. Many unusual varieties and

old time favorites. There is also a nice selection of bulbs and perennial plants.

Sooner Plant Farm, Inc

25976 S. 524 Rd.

Park Hill, OK 74451

Tel.: (918)453-077

Southern Exposure Seed Exchange

PO Box 460

Mineral, VA 23117

Phone: 540-894-9480

Fax: 540-894-9481

Annuals

Bulbs

Perennials

Exotic Plants and Flowers

Flower, Vegetable and Wildflower Seeds

Fruit Trees and Berries

Garden Supplies, Tools and Power Equipment

Gifts and Decorative Accessories

Ground Covers, Shrubs, Trees, and Vines

Herbs and Vegetables

Irrigation Supplies and Equipment

Fertilizer, Weed & Pest Control Products

Magazines and Books

Ornamental Grasses and Plants

Other

We are a wonderful source for vegetables selected in a day where taste and local adaptability were the primary factors. We have an extensive line of heirloom and other open pollinated seeds and seed saving supplies. Many of our varieties are certified organic. We also carry a wide variety of garlic and perennial onion bulbs and medicinal herb rootstock. We are a source for naturally colored cotton seeds. Many of our products are Certified Organic.

Website: www.southernexposure.com

Email Contact: gardens@southernexposure.com

SpringHill

110 West Elm St.

Tipp City, OH 45371

1-513-354-1509

www.springhillnursery.com

52 pages

This catalog is loaded with perennials of all kinds. It has ground covers, grasses, clematis and much more. There is even a page of Bonsai trees. There is a nice rose section, ornamemtal trees and shrubs.

Stark Bro's

P.O. Box 1800

Louisiana, MO 63353

Email: info@starkbros.com

Phone: 800.325.4180

http://www.starkbros.com/

Swallowtail Garden Seeds

122 Calistoga Road, #178

Santa Rosa, CA 95409

Phone: Toll Free 1-877-489-7333

707-538-3585

http://www.swallowtailgardenseeds.com/

Siskiyou Rare Plant Nursery

2825 Cummings Rd.

Medford, OR 97501

(541) 772-6846. $3

http://siskiyourareplantnursery.com/

Tater-Mater Seeds

PO Box 16085

Seattle, WA 98116

http://tatermaterseeds.com/shop/

Territorial Seed Company

PO Box 158

Cottate Grove, OR 97424

1-541-942-9547

www.territorialseed.com

This is a good catalog for market gardeners. Territoral has a
big selection of vegetables. There are a lot of different
varieties of beans, with 25 pound bags available many
varieties. Sweet and popcorn also well represented. Many
varieties of lettuce also listed. Melons, peppers, peas,
pumpkins and squash, along with boatloads of tomatoes.
They also have a large selecion of annual flowers, available
in larger quantities, so small greenhouse growers would find
this catalog helpful. There are approximately 30 varieties of
sunflowers, and lots of herbs. There is a good selection of

growing supplies, including several types of spun bond fabric row covers. You will find a pretty good selection of organic growing aids in here also. Also a small selection of honey bee supplies, including a mason bee starter kit.

Thompson and Morgan

220 Faraday Ave

Jackson NJ 08527

1-800-274-7333

www.thompsonandmorgan.com

200 pages of pure joy! Thompson and Morgan is one of the most complete seed catalogs available to the home gardener. You will find something of everything including the most popular annual and perennial flowers, vegetables and herbs, tree seeds and houseplants. There are hard to find varieties, standard varieties and some downright odd and unusual varieties. This catalog focuses on seeds, so you won't find many gardening supplies. Thompson and Morgan is one seed catalog the serious gardener shouldn't be without.

Totally Tomatoes

334 West Stroud Street

Randolph, WI 53956

1-800-345-5977

www.totallytomato.com

41 pages of nothing but tomatoes. They have the standard varieties available everywhere like Burpee Big Boy and Park Whopper. But there are many hard to find varieties like Aunt Ruby's German Green, Dixie Golden Giant and Bloody

Butcher. They also have a good selection of peppers , salad greens and cucumbers.

Vermont Bean Seed Company

334 W Stroud Street

Randolph, WI 53956

800-349-1071

www.vermontbean.com

79 page catalog.

These folks really do have the beans, sixteen pages of them. The catalog is

chuck full of other stuff, too. Vegetable seeds are in good supply as well as some flower seeds and herbs. They also sell vegetable and flower plants. Garden supplies include a nice selection of organic garden aids, and seed starting supplies.

Viette, Andre, Farm & Nursery,

Rt. 1, Box 16,

Fishersville, VA 22939.

(703) 943-2315. $3

http://www.viette.com/

Wayside Gardens

1 Garden Lane

Hodges, SC 29695-0001

1-800-845-1124

www.waysidegardens.com

164 pages

Wayside Gardens is an exclusively nursery stock catalog with extensive offerings of perennials, roses, shrubbery and ornamental trees. Many offerings are exclusive to them, or hard to find plants. This is the catalog for the discriminating gardener who is looking for the new, unusual, or unique.

Wildseed Farms

425 Wildflower Hills

PO Box 3000

Fredericksburg TX 78624-3000

1-800-848-0078

www.wildseedfarms.com

50 Pages

The catalog contains extensive instructions about how to establish wildflower stands. There are regional wildflower mixes as well as selections of individual wildflowers. Seeds are available in small gardener sized packets as well as bulk quantities suitable for large plantings. There is also a section of native grasses.

Mossy Feet Books Catalog

To Get Your Free Copy of the Mossy Feet Books Catalogue, go to www.mossyfeet.com and click the catalogue link.

Gardening Books

Abe's Guide to Growing the Tomato

The Solar Garden

Abe's Guide To The Peony

Abe's Guide to The Lanceleaf Coreopsis

Abe's Guide To The Threadleaf Coreopsis

Abe's Guide To The Creeping Phlox

Abe's Guide To The Hibiscus

Abe's Guide to Wall Germander

Abe's Guide To The Bearded Iris

Abe's Guide to the Chrysanthemum

Abe's Guide to the Fall Garden

Abe's Guide To Perennial Candytuft

Abe's Guide to Making Compost

Abe's Guide to Botany

Abe's Guide To Plant Stems

Abe's Guide to Buddleia

Abe's Guide to Leaves

Abe's Guide to Blanket Flower

Abe's Guide to Blackberry Lily

Abe's Guide to Flowers

Abe's Guide to Perennial Balloon Flower

Abe's Guide to Perennial Alyssum

Brilliant yellow blossoms and evergreen foliage make perennial alyssum a must for every perennial garden.

Abe's Guide to the Plant Root

The Complete Guide to the Plant Seeds

The Guide to Robotic Vacuum Cleaners

Abe's Guide to September/October Wildflowers

Abe's Guide to August Wildflowers

Abe's Guide to July Wildflowers

Abe's Guide to June Wildflowers

Abe's Guide to May Wildflowers

Abe's Guide to April Wildflowers

Abe's Guide to Growing Marigolds

Abe's Guide to Full Sun Perennials

Fantasy Books

Fading Photographs

Calls After Midnight

The Pirate King

Bearl's First Test

Heir of the Pirate King

Rise of the Pirate King

Tarque's Search

The Fall of Acerland

Legend of the Wizard Tarque

Covenant's Peril

Tale of the Crystal Eye

Flea Market Tales – Collection 1

The Wine Goblet

Box of Secrets

Lament of Arii

Glade of Death

Before the Storm

Gault

The Order of Solaun

Radio Memories

Seven Day Clock

Revealed by the Light

Zerena

Restoration

Time of Troubles

War of the Crystal

The Oasis

Pillars of Borr

Turmoil

Awakening

Demon Soul

Barn of Fear

Ten Tales for the Campfire

Five Tales for the Campfire – Volume Two

Halloween Party

The Dinner Bell Rings at Midnight

The Sinkhole

The Woman in the Wind

Tale of the White Rock

Field of Snakes

What's in the Cooler, Mister?

The Covenant

Five Tales for the Campfire

Promise of the White Rock

The Skull Garden

The Hungry House

Appointment

The Rise of Gwaum

Pets

Footsteps

Gandy Rand – Erotic

Short Stories and Collections

Double Trouble

Motorcycle Ride

Mrs. Boswell

Sales Call

Slow Day

Five Erotic Stories Collection 1

Mile High Club

Euchre Game

Masquerade Ball

Candy Store

Special Delivery

Five Erotic Stories Collection 2

Five Erotic Stories Complete Collection

Humor Books

Stroke and Counterstroke

Five Stories From the Liar's Bench

Screams in the Night

Old Cameras Never Die

Whose Kidneys Are These, Anyway?

Practical Joke

Ad Space

Ten Funny Stories Complete Collection

Five Funny Stories – Volume II

Dog Ballooning

Holey Boat

Bring Your Pet to Work Day

An Ode to the Big Toe

Toe Tag

Five Funny Stories

Hole to China

One Fine Morning on Mulberry Lane

Perfect Afternoon

Truffle Shop Tale

The Adventures of Toby and Wilbur Complete Short Story Collection

Toby and Wilbur Bear– Legend of the Christmas Train

Toby and Wilbur and the Legend of the Trestletown Ghost

Toby and Wilber - The Great Kite Caper

Toby and Wilbur Bear – 3, 2, 1, Blastoff

Toby and Wilbur Bear – The Great Bear Race

Rich Woman's Dog

Bernie Fuller though life as a rich woman's dog would be a hoot.

Toby and Wilbur Bear – The Amazing Hovercraft Adventure

Toby and Wilbur – The Second Day

Toby and Wilbur – The Beginning Begins

Science Fiction Books

Solar Power Primer

Alternative Energy Sources

Five Science Fiction Short Stories - Volume II

Ten Science Fiction Short Stories

Signals

Spores

Mind Games

Biology Experiment

The Database

Secretary General

Five Science Fiction Short Stories

Ad Campaign

The Smoke

The Elixir

Unacceptable Use of Resources

Down the Barrel of a Gun

Semi-Autobiographical Books

Ten Ricky Huening Stories

Five Ricky Huening Stories – Collection II

1963

People Are Like Peanuts

Clay Rockets

Cookie

The Crick

Five Ricky Huening Stories – Collection I

Hauling Out the Trash

The Time Machine

The Chicken House

The Magic Swing

The Shoe Fence

Travel Books

The Hawaiian Chronicles – Our Hawaiian Cruise Adventures

The Alaska Chronicles – Our Alaskan Cruise Adventure

Indiana State Park Series

A Visit to Pokagon State Park, Indiana

A Visit to the Falls of the Ohio

A Visit to the Land of Lincoln, Indiana

A Visit to Harmonie State Park, Indiana

A Visit to Brown County State Park

A Visit to Spring Mill State Park

History Books

History Books

Two New Series Debut Late 2015

Travels Through Indiana History – Indiana History Daytrips

Indiana History Markers, Sites, Museums and More

A Daily Historical Fact Collection about Indiana

Indiana Bicentennial History Series

Indiana History Day in History Series – 2015 Edition

American History A Year at A Time – 2015 Edition

American History A Day at A Time – December 2015 Edition

American History A Day at A Time – November 2015 Edition

American History A Day at A Time – October 2015 Edition

American History A Day at A Time – September 2015 Edition

American History A Day at A Time – August 2015 Edition

American History A Day at A Time – July 2015 Edition

American History A Day at A Time – June 2015 Edition

American History A Day at A Time – May 2015 Edition

American History A Day at A Time – April 2015 Edition

American History A Day at A Time – March 2015 Edition

American History A Day at A Time – February 2015 Edition

American History A Day at A Time – January 2015 Edition

A Short History of the Game Of Chess

A Brief History of Candle Making

A Short History of Coins

A Short History of the United States Constitution

A Short History of Kites

A Short History of Transportation

Formation and Structure of the Seed in Angiosperms

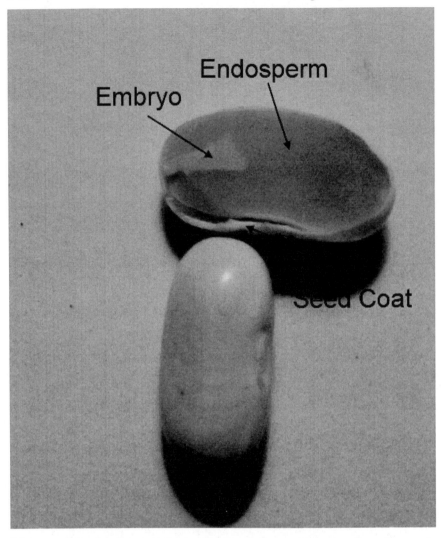

This article deals strictly with seed formation in the class of plants called angiosperms, or "enclosed seeds." It also deals with the further division of the dicots, or plants with two seed leaves.

The seed is the structure which develops from the fertilized ovule of the flower. The seed comprises all of the genetic information required to produce a new plant like the plant from which it originated. It is composed of three distinct structures, the embryo, the endosperm and the seed coat. The formation of these structures occurs during the process called fertilization. Fertilization occurs, as it does with all flowering plants, after a grain of pollen, produced by the anther of a flower, lands on the stigma of a flower of the same species. When this occurs the pollen grains grow a tube which extends down through the style into the ovary. The sperm cells from the pollen travel down the tube and then fuse with the nuclei of an egg cell that is within the ovary.

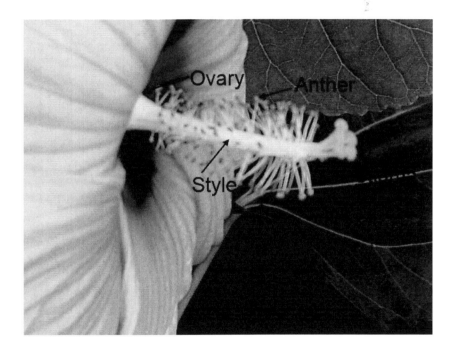

In angiosperms double fertilization occurs during this process. One fertilization method involves the fusion of sperm cell nuclei with an egg cell. This part of the fertilization forms the zygote which develops into a pro zygote and then into the embryo. A secondary fertilization involves second sperm cell nuclei and the polar nuclei. This fertilization forms the endosperm.

This double fertilization has formed two of the three parts of the seed, the embryo and the endosperm. The seed coat develops over the endosperm and the embryo, protecting them from the elements and holding the parts together.

A zygote is the cell, which forms after sexual fertilization, occurs. This zygote contained within the seed is the undeveloped plant and within it is all the genetic information needed for the plant to grow. This genetic information, or DNA, comes from both parent plants which contributed to the initial fertilization. If self fertilization has occurred, which happens in many types of plants, the genetic material comes from a single plant. After formation of the seed the zygote develops into a pro zygote which then develops into the embryo. The embryo becomes inactive, waiting for conditions to become satisfactory for germination. Depending upon the plant species and storage conditions a zygote can remain in this inactive state for a period of hours to many, many years after the seed forms. Some plant seeds will germinate immediately after they fall from the plant. Other plant seeds will need a complicated series of developments to trigger germination. The zygote consists of two portions, one of which will form the stem and leaves. The other portion will form the root of the plant. In dicot plants there are two seed leaves present which will emerge upon germination and produce food for the plant until the true leaves develop.

The endosperm is quick to develop after fertilization. Once the endosperm develops it too will remain inactive until after germination occurs. The purpose of the endosperm in the seed structure is to serve as a food source for the embryo to use once germination begins. The embryo will draw upon this food source until the roots and the leaves develop well enough to draw nutrients from the soil and gather light from the sun and manufacture the food the plant needs to survive.

The seed coat's purpose in the structure of the seed is to protect the embryo and endosperm. Seed coats develop from the ovule of the flower and it will remain in place until germination occurs. The seed coat sheds off at this point. Once the seed forms it enters a state of dormancy. Dormancy can last for hours, days, weeks or years, depending upon the species of the plants and its growth requirements.

Find them on **www.mossyfeetbooks.com**

Printed in Great Britain
by Amazon